A CALL TO ARMS

YOUR QUICK START TO FIGHT LIKE HEAVEN!

DRENDA KEESEE

CONTENTS

INTRODUCTION

The war is on! The days are getting darker, and God has called every man, woman, and child to be on guard, stand firm in the faith, and occupy until Jesus Christ returns. It's time to fight like heaven and kick hell out!

There are seven mountains of influence that control the world around us: Religion, economy/business, health/medicine, media/entertainment, government/politics, education, and family. Popular speaker, life coach, pastor, businesswoman, television host of *Drenda*, YouTube host of the Drenda on Guard channel, and best-selling author Drenda Keesee has recently been leading the charge to take on these mountains and to empower the church to fight with her.

In her *Fight Like Heaven! A Cultural Guide to Living on Guard (Fight Like Heaven!)* book, Drenda leaves no stone unturned as she uncovers and exposes the enemy's last days' agenda and last resort to ensnare, enslave, impoverish, and destroy humankind in order to usher in the New World Order, which is nothing but a doomed counterfeit to the coming Kingdom of Jesus Christ!

From the United Nations to the World Economic Forum (WEF) to the COVID-19 deception, Drenda covers a multitude of topics in great depth in *Fight Like Heaven!*, including: the Fourth Industrial Revolution, the Great Reset, and the New World Order; the elite's sinister plan of transhumanism; the religious world's involvement in the New World Order; the origins and pervasiveness of occultism and secret societies within our modern culture; financial schemes designed to enslave us; the effect of government, organized medicine, and the pharmaceutical industry on medicine and health; schools, hospitals, and big business advancement of the LGBTQ+ agenda among children; the media's control and manipulation of information to drive the enemy's agenda; biblical Scriptures for living on guard; biblical prophecies of the last days and Jesus Christ's return; and so much more!

Fight Like Heaven! not only reveals the schemes that empower institutions and ensnare people but is also full of strategies, Scriptures, and wise counsel to equip God's children to engage in the war against darkness, live on guard, and take back the mountains of infuence for the Kingdom of God!

This *A CALL TO ARMS: Your Quick Start to Fight Like Heaven!* guide is designed to supplement and enhance your study of *Fight Like Heaven!* Within this Call to Arms, you will find a brief teaching on each of the seven mountains, specific instructions for spiritual warfare and intercession over these areas, and recommendations for personal strategies you can take to tangibly impact these spheres for the Kingdom of God. Before diving into the specific mountains, this guide will provide an abbreviated overview of spiritual warfare basics and the New World Order, which are more fully covered in the *Fight Like Heaven! A Cultural Guide to Living on Guard* book.

Let's get started!

1

SPIRITUAL WARFARE BASICS

Praise be to the Lord my Rock, who trains my hands for war, my fingers for battle.

—Psalm 144:1 (NIV)

The most basic foundational truth we need to grasp to reclaim the seven mountains is to understand these four basic principles: 1) God is good; 2) Satan is evil; 3) God has power over the enemy; and 4) He's given you the power over Satan. While the first three principles of spiritual warfare are generally accepted among believers, the fourth one has been lost on much of the church. You need only look in your Bible; it has been there all along!

And God raised us up with Christ and seated us with him in the heavenly realms in Christ Jesus, in order that in the coming ages he might show the incomparable riches of his grace, expressed in his kindness to us in Christ Jesus.

—Ephesians 2:6-7 (NIV)

Jesus said:

> *I will give you the keys of the kingdom of heaven; whatever you bind on earth will be bound in heaven, and whatever you loose [release] on earth will be loosed [released] in heaven.*
>
> —Matthew 16:19a (NIV)

> *I have given you authority to trample on snakes and scorpions and to overcome all the power of the enemy.*
>
> —Luke 10:19 (NIV)

> *These works and greater works shall you do because I go to my Father.*
>
> —John 14:12b (NKJV)

Jesus has given you His same authority by restoring the dominion decree of Genesis 1:26.

> *Then God said, "Let us make man in Our image, according to Our likeness; <u>let them have dominion</u> over the fish of sea, over the birds of the air, and over the cattle, <u>over all the earth</u> and over every creeping thing that creeps on the earth."*
>
> —Genesis 1:26 (NKJV)

While Adam surrendered this authority to Satan in the Garden of Eden, man's dominion was returned through Christ, through whom we *"have been brought to fullness"* since *"He is the head over every power and authority"* (Colossians 2:10b, NIV).

Jesus then gave that same authority to us, His church (Luke 10:19, NIV). The Bible says we are *"heirs of God and co-heirs with Christ"* (Romans 8:17)! In fact, you are seated with Christ in heavenly places far above all principality, might, and dominion (Ephesians 1:20-21, 2:6, NIV).

So how do we go about enforcing our authority? First, we must remember that "*the one who is in you is greater than the one who is in the world*," i.e., Satan (1 John 4:4b, NIV).

Ephesians 6:10-12 (NIV) tell us to:

> *Finally, be strong in the Lord and in his mighty power. Put on the full armor of God, so that you can take your stand against the devil's schemes. For our struggle is not against flesh and blood, but against the rulers, against the authorities, against the powers of this dark world and against the spiritual forces of evil in the heavenly realms.*

Likewise, 2 Corinthians 10:4 (NIV) reminds us that:

> *The weapons we fight with are not the weapons of the world. On the contrary, they have divine power to demolish strongholds.*

These authorities, dark powers, spiritual forces, and strongholds are a hierarchy of demonic forces that try to oppose mankind, to steal, kill, and destroy. These lawbreakers wreak havoc on mankind, including unsuspecting Christians who do not understand their authority in Christ or the laws of His Kingdom. There is no need to beg and plead for God to help us when Jesus has already defeated the enemy and given us the keys of His Kingdom. We simply need to exercise our dominion and engage in spiritual warfare by strategic prayer, declaring God's Word, following the Holy Spirit, walking in faith, and taking action!

2

THE NEW WORLD ORDER

For there is nothing hidden that will not be disclosed, and nothing concealed that will not be known or brought out into the open.

—Luke 8:17 (NIV)

Before we delve into each of the seven mountains, it is essential that you understand that these mountains are now dominated by the Antichrist spirit and the evil hearts of proud men. They are converging toward one nefarious end goal—the establishment of the New World Order. The details of this one world government are set forth in *Fight Like Heaven! A Cultural Guide to Living on Guard*, which you are strongly encouraged to study.

What is the New World Order? Like every facet of life, the Bible tells us! Primarily through the books of Revelation, Daniel, Ezekiel, Matthew, and 2 Thessalonians, biblical prophecy reveals that a great political, military, and economic superpower will arise in the last days—the Antichrist—and set up a system of a one world government. This one world government will be led by the "dragon," Satan, and will be a mere *counterfeit* of the coming Kingdom of Jesus

Christ. It is the "anti-Kingdom." Always remember, Satan creates *nothing*; he is unoriginal and can only imitate, never duplicate!

When are the plans for the New World Order? Over the last few decades, we have heard countless world leaders and American Presidents fondly refer to the New World Order, starting with George H.W. Bush in 1990. Most recently, Joe Biden said on March 21, 2022 that there would be "a new world order" established and led by the United States: "You know, we are at an inflection point, I believe, in the world economy—not just the world economy, in the world. ... As one of the top military people said to me in a security meeting the other day, 60 million people died between 1900 and 1946, and since then, we've established *a liberal world order*, and that hadn't happened in a long while.... There's going to be a *new world order* out there. We've got to lead it, and we've got to unite the rest of the free world in doing it."[1] Thus, there is no doubt that the plans for a New World Order are well underway and have been for quite some time.

Who are the major players? While Satan is obviously the power behind this "anti-Kingdom," he uses people and worldly institutions to accomplish his purposes. At the forefront of this plan are as follows: the United Nations, the World Economic Forum, the World Health Organization, Klaus Schwab, Yuval Noah Harari, George Soros, Bill Gates, and all WEF-aligned companies, including Google, Amazon, BlackRock, Dell Technologies, GE, Intel, Meta, Microsoft, Johnson & Johnson, Pfizer, PayPal, UBS, and Visa, to name only a few. Their slogans—New Normal, Great Reset, and Build Back Better—are indistinguishable and all synonymous with the New World Order. Similarly, their causes and buzz words— globalism, environmentalism, open borders, climate change,

---

1 Brianna Lyman, "Biden: 'There's Going to Be a New World Order,'" *Daily Caller*, https://www.dailycaller.com, March 21, 2022.

sustainability, social equity, gender identity, wealth redistribution, population control, gene editing and/or transhumanism—are all New World Order lexicons, which should put you on alert.

While to the unsuspecting they present themselves as angels of light, the truth is that they see people and lands as property to control and exploit. Notably, every agenda they push is directly contradicted by the Word of God. As the prophet Isaiah warned, they *"call evil good and good evil"* (Isaiah 5:20, NIV).

While their plans for humankind are for war, famine, poverty, and depopulation, rest assured that those who perpetrate crimes on God's men, women, and children will not get away with it! When the armies of the world wage war upon Israel, Jesus Christ, the Anointed One, with an incredible army, will descend into the battle and strike down His enemies. The blood will run deep and will vindicate the saints of God. No evil deed will go unpunished.

Jesus will return, and He will set up His Kingdom, the stone that crushes them all, and make the kingdoms of the world the kingdoms of our God. The millennial reign of Christ as King on Earth will be the day of rest in the physical realm as it was placed in the spiritual realm at His first coming. The long-awaited coming of Christ is at hand. Prophetic events are all in place. Jesus came in humility and died, but His next coming will be a triumphant entry of the King of kings, where He will appear as a Conqueror at the helm of heaven's armies.

> *Then the seventh angel blew his trumpet, and there were loud voices in heaven, saying, "The kingdom of the world has become the kingdom of our Lord and of his Christ, and he shall reign forever and ever."*
>
> —Revelation 11:15 (ESV)

This is an exciting time to live and take the mountains to influence others for Christ through your life. Your life and time were determined by God, and He chose you for this time!

3

RELIGION

Occupy till I come.

—Luke 19:13b (KJV)

Christianity, with 2.3 billion professed followers, is the largest religion in the world today and, geographically, the most widespread. Nevertheless, we are witnessing nations rebelling against God and His people as never before. Christianity has been mocked, scorned, censored, and silenced on every mountain. In fact, more Christians have been killed for their faith over the last 100 years than in all the previous centuries combined.

In some ways, the church bears responsibility for abandoning the six other mountains to pursue religion alone. Business, government, family, media, arts/entertainment, education, *and* religion influence our society. Unfortunately, when we vacate these opportunities or allow an increasingly hostile culture to minimize our involvement, what fills the void of what was once a vibrant life-producing faith is secularism, atheism, occultism, or dead religion. All are empty.

We miss opportunities to influence society when the true church of

Jesus Christ is not present in every sphere. This is what Jesus referred to when He said, *"Occupy till I come."* This is a military reference to "take territory, invade, and take over." Jesus was speaking of world impact!

What are we to occupy, and what territory are we to take? Everything and everywhere—all seven mountains! This is the dominion God first spoke of in Genesis 1:26b (KJV), *"Let them have dominion ... over all the earth."* Remember that Jesus, the last Adam, returned man's dominion through His resurrection. Jesus *"Having disarmed the powers and authorities, he [Jesus] made a public spectacle of them, triumphing over them by the cross"* (Colossians 2:15, NIV).

As the church, we have dominion authority! As part of this dominion decree, Jesus told us to:

> *"Go and make disciples of <u>all nations</u>, baptizing them in the name of the Father and of the Son and of the Holy Spirit, and teaching them to obey everything I have commanded you."*
> —Matthew 28:19-20a (NIV)

Jesus likewise said:

> *"On this rock I will build My church, and the gates of Hades shall not prevail against it. And I will give you the keys of the kingdom of heaven, and whatever you bind on earth will be bound in heaven, and whatever you loose on earth will be loosed in heaven."*
> —Matthew 16:18b-19 (NKJV)

Is there any question that the church, which possesses the keys of the Kingdom, and against which Hades' gates are defenseless, was to take territory on a global scale to bring God's will to Earth as it is in heaven? Especially on the mountain of religion? Instead, members of the church have compromised their theology, particularly concerning sexuality, family, economics, and morality. Some churches have closed their doors, and other prominent religious organizations have joined together with powerful world alliances to advance global agendas under the guise of religion—but void of biblical truth.

Jesus warned against a form of godliness but without His power. Religion is simply the dead remains of what used to be alive. When Christ is no longer the rightful head of the body, man and his plans take over and produce an apostate church. Jesus said, "*Because you are … neither cold nor hot, I will spew you out of my mouth*" (Revelation 3:16b, RSV). We, the church, cannot settle for being lukewarm! No one was ever transformed by a lukewarm gospel. People want change, and we know the change they need that can transform the culture just like it has throughout history—a vibrant, red-hot faith that changes lives and nations.

There must be a purpose attached to our faith, and every believer must be on a Kingdom assignment in some area of impact. It is your mission, as a member of the body of Christ, to share the Kingdom by example and in your unique assignment, whether it's a call to ministry, politics, music, arts, business, media, medicine, education, or motherhood. We can infiltrate the seven mountains again—with the right mindset—and reclaim lost or missed opportunities. It is time to take our dominion authority!

Spiritual Warfare and Strategic Prayer:

➢ Personally and on behalf of the church repent for abdicating our God-given dominion to occupy all seven mountains and for advancing or tolerating a compromised, worldly, lukewarm gospel contrary to the one proclaimed by Jesus Christ.

➢ Pray for a mighty move of the Holy Spirit that causes a fiery revival and awakening in the church to take dominion, preach the Gospel, and make disciples of nations!

➢ Cut the church's ties with every spiritual connection to occultism, paganism, and Babylonian gods that have infiltrated and tainted the church. Pray that the Lord will cleanse the church from all defilement so that the church, His Bride, may present herself as radiant, holy, and blameless.

➢ Pray for a renewed hunger for God's Word, a thirst for righteousness, and a desire for boldness within the body of Christ.

➢ Cast down all spirits of religion and false gods that blind mankind to the truth of Jesus Christ.

➢ Bind all oppressive, mocking, and persecuting spirits that silence or censor the church.

➢ Call forth opportunities, individually and within the body of Christ, to attain influence among the seven mountains.

➢ Pray that church leaders would become disentangled from the culture and have discernment and wisdom on how to minister truth to a lost and dying world.

➢ Declare that the church will be the salt and light of the earth as Scripture proclaims!

Call to Arms:

➢ Ask the Holy Spirit to reveal any areas where you have accepted and/or advanced a compromised or watered-down gospel, especially in the areas of sexuality, family, finances, and morality, then study what the Bible says about these matters.

➢ What mountain of influence were you created to infiltrate? (The answer will become more clear as you study this guide.)

➢ Are you exercising your dominion authority in your daily life, including your prayer life? How so? In what areas could you be stronger and bolder?

➢ Are you tenaciously pursuing God's assignment for your life? If not, why not?

➢ If you are uncertain of your God-given mission (both in work and in ministry), ask the Lord to show you His plans for your life. Be mindful that God brings us new assignments based on the season of life we are in and as we mature and trust in Him.

➢ What ways can you demonstrate the Kingdom and "occupy" in your unique assignment? Ask the Lord for divine creativity and opportunities.

➢ How can you support your pastors and church leaders in taking territory for the Kingdom in your communities and even on a global scale?

4

BUSINESS/ECONOMY

For the Lord your God will bless you, as he promised you, and you shall lend to many nations, but you shall not borrow, and you shall rule over many nations, but they shall not rule over you.

—Deuteronomy 15:6 (ESV)

From the earliest times, people have struggled under an earth curse system of financial bondage. The Bible says that "*The rich rules over the poor and the borrower is the slave of the lender*" (Proverbs 22:7, ESV). America, or rather its citizens and future generations, is saddled with over $30 trillion in debt[2] with a present borrowing cap of $31.4 trillion,[3] inflation is at its highest rate in 40 years,[4] and

2 Peter G. Peterson Foundation, "The National Debt Is Now More Than $30 Trillion. What Does That Mean?" https://www.pgpf.org/infographic/the-national-debt-is-now-more-than-30-trillion-what-does-that-mean, February 1, 2022.

3 Paul Grant, "Biden Signs Bill Raising U.S. Debt Limit into Law - White House," Reuters, December 26. 2021.

4 Christopher Rugaber, "US Inflation Highest in 40 years, with No Let-up in Sight," https://www.abcnewsgo.com, February 10, 2022.

the price of gasoline has increased more than 100% since 2020.[5] [6] The power of our current administration's policies, compounding interest, and the wiles of a banking industry threaten the American standard of life as we know it.

Devious powers are playing America for a collapse financially and a Great Reset. The creation of the Federal Reserve (which is neither federal nor a reserve), the removal of the gold standard, and the printing of money with no value attached but an IOU and a dollar, unbacked by any commodity or asset, place America in her most vulnerable state ever.

In Klaus Schwab and Thierry Malleret's book, *COVID-19: The Great Reset*, Schwab reveals the globalists' vision and expectation for the US dollar, stating:

> For decades, the US has enjoyed the "exorbitant privilege" of retaining the global currency reserve, a status that has long been "a perk of imperial might and an economic elixir." To a considerable extent, American power and prosperity have been built and reinforced by the global trust in the dollar and the willingness of customers abroad to hold it, most often in the form of US government bonds. …For quite some time, some analysts and policy-makers have been considering a possible and progressive end to the dominance of the dollar. They now think the [COVID] pandemic might be the catalyst that proves them right…. [D]oubters of the US dollar's dominance point to

---

5 "The U.S. Economy & Inflation: What You Need to Know to Protect Your Money," Drenda on Guard, https://www.youtube.com/watch?v=MUiw5ygOrkQ, March 11, 2022.
6 Robert Burgess, Elaine He, and Eliza Winger, "How Close Are We Really to 1970s-Style Inflation?" https://www.bloomberg.com, June 11, 2022.

the incompatibility of its status as a global reserve currency with rising economic nationalism at home.[7]

In other words, Schwab and his faction are advocating for a reset of American dominance and independence (the last and most powerful obstacle they face) and threatening that the failure of the US to relinquish its nationalism and succumb to globalism puts the dollar—and thus the American economy—at risk of implosion. Just recently, the WEF seemingly celebrated the fact that "the share of US dollar reserves held by central banks fell to 59 percent—its lowest level in 25 years—during the fourth quarter of 2020."[8] Given the dollar's status as fiat currency, the national debt, the economic decline of the US' GDP in successive quarters, and the world rooting against us, does America have any hope?

Yes, but only if America aligns with Scripture. The Bible says:

> *No one can serve two masters. Either you will hate the one and love the other, or you will be devoted to the one and despise the other. You cannot serve both God and money.*
> —Matthew 6:24 (NIV)

The enemy wants God's people to serve money rather than God's purposes. This is why he has infiltrated the US economy with the false gospels of poverty and debt. If he can cripple us economically, he can rob us individually and as a nation of God's blessings and plans. We must face the fact that his ultimate plan is to draw us into the New World Order through economic collapse.

---

7 Klaus Schwab and Thierry Malleret, *COVID-19: The Great Reset*, Forum Publishing, 2020, pgs. 32-33.

8 https://www.weforum.org/agenda/2021/05/us-dollar-share-of-global-foreign-exchange-reserves-drops-to-25-year-low

Instead, God has called us to "*Give, and it will be given to you. A good measure, pressed down, shaken together and running over, will be poured into your lap*" (Luke 6:38, NIV). In fact, in our obedience by tithing, God invites us to "test" Him "*and see if [He] will not throw open the floodgates of heaven and pour out so much blessing that there will not be room enough to store it*" (Malachi 3:10b, NIV). God promises to add all of these things (our wants and needs), but we must "*seek first the kingdom of God and his righteousness*" (Matthew 6:33, NKJV).

As individuals, we must get our financial houses in order so we can rise above the enemy's plan and be ready to reach a dying world with His love and provision. Furthermore, as Kingdom businessmen and entrepreneurs, we are called to invade the mountain of business and economics, which is currently occupied by corporations hailing allegiance to the New World Order. However, we as Christ's followers have an advantage: "*If God is for us, who can be against us*" (Romans 8:31b, NIV)? Because the Kingdom of God is within us as believers, the direction we need to thrive in hard economic times will flow out of our spirits. The Kingdom of God is not subject to this world's economy, but we must depend on strategies from the Holy Spirit to prosper in these times.

Spiritual Warfare and Strategic Prayer:

➢ Acknowledge God as your provider and thank Him that He meets all of your needs according to the riches of His glory in Christ Jesus.

➢ Pull down and destroy the spirits of the Antichrist, Baal, greed, poverty, and slavery now at work in the earth.

➢ Curse the plans for a New World Order, one world government, Great Reset, or any other contrived, counterfeit kingdom of Satan.

➢ Proclaim that God's people will be free from the agendas of globalists and secret societies and that all of their works done in darkness will be brought to light.

➢ Declare that these wicked men's source of wealth and supply will be completely cut off and stored up for the righteous.

➢ Declare that the US will reimplement a monetary system with asset backed currency and establish sound economic legislation and policy.

➢ Pray that God's people will receive a revelation of the Kingdom laws of sowing and reaping, giving and receiving.

➢ Pray that God will raise up and advance Kingdom businessmen and entrepreneurs to prosper and support the economy in these times.

Call to Arms:

➢ Seek first the Kingdom of God and His righteousness.

➢ Give tithes regularly, and give offerings by faith targeted for your specific needs.

➢ Ask the Holy Spirit to give you creative ideas for businesses or ventures that allow you to be free from dependence on large corporations for income.

➤ If your vocation makes you financially vulnerable in this economic climate, pray that God will create a new career path for you to use your talents and achieve financial security.

➤ Get out of debt, and stay out of debt!

➤ Choose Kingdom businesses and small businesses to purchase goods and services from rather than large retailers.

➤ Support Kingdom politicians with sound economy policies; voice your concerns to those holding office to effectuate change.

5

HEALTH/MEDICINE

All the nations were deceived by your sorcery [pharmakeia].
—Revelation 18:23b (CSB)

Although the COVID-19 pandemic has certainly infected all of the seven mountains, its threat was ostensibly about health, right? Yes, but it has had nothing to do with protecting our health. It was about exploiting it for sinister purposes. Make no mistake. Everything about COVID-19, from its origins to its containment to its treatment, has been a matter of mass public deception. President Biden, who is "fully vaccinated" and twice boosted, assured the American public on multiple occasions, "You're not going to get COVID if you have these vaccinations."[9] He has recently tested positive for COVID. Dr. Anthony Fauci, the individual largely responsible for the COVID lockdown of our country in 2020 and the National Institute of Health's funding of the Wuhan Institute from which the virus originated, has likewise recently tested positive

9 Alvin Woodward and Hope Yen, "AP FACT CHECK: Biden Goes Too Far in Assurances on Vaccines," https://apnews.com/article/joe-biden-business-health-government-and-politics-coronavirus-pandemic-46a270ce0f681caa7e4143e2ae9a0211, July 22, 2021.

for COVID. He, the most prominent advocate of the COVID-19 vaccine, was also vaccinated and twice boosted.

Recent studies of the COVID-19 vaccine by MRNA researchers have revealed "evidence that vaccination induces a profound impairment in type one interferon signaling, which has diverse adverse consequences to human health" and "potential profound disturbances in regulatory control of protein synthesis and cancer surveillance… These disturbances potentially have a causal link to neurodegenerative disease… myocarditis, Bell's Palsy, liver disease, impaired adaptive immunity, impaired DNA damage response, etc." following the COVID vaccine.[10] *The Lancet*, one of the most famous scientific journals in the world, published a study that "showed that immune function among vaccinated individuals 8 months after the administration of two doses of COVID-19 vaccine was lower than that among the unvaccinated individuals" and "[a]s a safety measure, further booster vaccinations should be discontinued."[11]

"The most recent data from the CDC shows that U.S. millennials, aged 25-44, experienced a record setting 84 percent increase in excess mortality during the final four months of 2021…. In all, excess death among those who are traditionally the healthiest Americans is up by an astonishing 84 percent. … Millennials were

10 Stephanie Seneff, Greg Nigh, Anthony M. Kyriakopoulos, Peter A. McCullough, "Innate Immune Suppression by SARS-CoV-2 mRNA Vaccinations: The Role of G-quadruplexes, Exosomes, and MicroRNAs," Food and Chemical Toxicology, Volume 164, June 2022, https://www.sciencedirect.com/science/article/pii/S027869152200206X?via%3Dihub.
11 Kenji Yamamoto, "Adverse Effects of COVID-19 Vaccines and Measures to Prevent Them," *Virology Journal* 19, 100 (2022), https://doi.org/10.1186/s12985-022-01831-0, citing Peter Nordström, Marcel Ballin, Anna Nordström, "Risk of Infection, Hospitalisation, and Death up to 9 Months after a Second Dose of COVID-19 Vaccine: a Retrospective, Total Population Cohort Study in Sweden," *The Lancet* 2022; 399: 814–23 Published online February 4, 2022, https://doi.org/10.1016/S0140-6736(22)00089-7.

by far hit hardest by the wave of excess deaths, likely because taking the jab was the only way for them to stay employed. Case in point, the excess deaths were almost seven times higher than those who are 85 or older."[12]

Perhaps even more disturbing than all the lies, financial devastation, sickness, injury, and death from the COVID vaccines is how easily most of the world was conned into serving themselves up as "hackable animals" to fulfill globalists' plans for transhumanism. *Fight Like Heaven!* discusses this subject in much more detail. To summarize, transhumanism is not only a belief but also a *goal* that human DNA can be improved by means of science and technology, i.e., genetic editing and technology injected into the body by way of "vaccines" and other devices.

These plans for transhumanism are not a conspiracy. The information is neither secret nor hidden. Through methods like the COVID vaccine, globalists are attempting to literally get under your skin to not only surveil you but also to modify your DNA through "genetic editing" and "hacking." Or even more chilling, they claim that humans can achieve immortality and "We don't need to wait for Jesus Christ to come back to Earth in order to overcome death. A couple of geeks in a laboratory can do it."[13] No! Our DNA is our God imprint, and eternal life can only be found through Jesus Christ.

Most assuredly, a day is coming when God will give us a new, glorified body that will restore all that was lost at the Fall when death entered, but transhumanism is Satan's counterfeit. We must not accept the counterfeit; we must never allow ourselves to be "hacked," "engineered," or mutated by the evil one.

12 Julian Conradson, "SHOCKING: Millennials Experienced the Worst-Ever Excess Mortality in History—An 84% Increase in Deaths After Vaccine Mandates Introduced," https://www.thegatewaypundit.com, March 19, 2022.
13 Yuval Noah Harari | "We Don't Need to Wait for Jesus Christ to Overcome Death," https://www.battleplan.news, April 28, 2022.

Spiritual Warfare and Strategic Prayer:

➢ Break and cast down the stronghold of the fear of death and disease in our land, the strategy of which is to exploit and harm humankind. Instead, declare faith and truth will prevail in the hearts of men.

➢ Curse COVID-19, monkeypox, and any other viral outbreaks, and declare that all plans to create or sustain future pandemics, lockdowns, and/or forced vaccinations will fail.

➢ Bind the Nephilim spirit that seeks to violate the seed of woman, whom the Lord prophesied would crush the head of the serpent, Satan, through the triumph of Jesus Christ.

➢ Curse the globalists' agendas for depopulation and transhumanism through "healthcare" or by any other means.

➢ Speak healing into the bodies of God's children who were forced or coerced to take the COVID-19 vaccine against their better judgment or faith, and declare that no weapon formed against them shall prosper!

➢ Rebuke and cast out the spirit of greed that dominates medical monopolies and pharmaceutical companies, and pray that the healthcare industry will be transformed to actually promote life and health.

Call to Arms:

➤ Ask the Holy Spirit to help you navigate through the propaganda, to discern the truth versus what others are telling you, even physicians, when it comes to your health. Be wary of those touting agendas.

➤ Beware of vaccines pushed in these last days, particularly those that are being administered pursuant to an "Emergency Use Authorization." The fact that vaccine manufacturers are essentially immune from liability resulting from injury or death should raise a huge red flag and compel you to do further research.

➤ If you are threatened by your employer to take a vaccine in violation of your faith or lose your job, consider seeking a religious exemption. Even if your employer pushes back, if enough employees object, your employer may change its policy. If unsuccessful, prayerfully seek God on a potential career or job change.

➤ Treat your body like the temple of the Holy Spirit that it is. It may be time to reevaluate your food choices, incorporate regular exercise, supplement with vitamins and minerals, and drink more water.

➤ If you are suffering from sickness or disease, know that God still heals today. The Bible instructs us to:

> *Call for the elders of the church and they are to pray over him, anointing him with oil in the name of the Lord, and the prayer of faith will restore the one who is sick.*
>
> —James 5:14-15a (NASB)

6

MEDIA

*And you were dead in the trespasses and sins in which you once walked, following the course of this world, following **the prince of the power of the air**, the spirit that is now at work in the sons of disobedience.*

—Ephesians 2:1-2 (ESV)

Today, the mountain of media is vast and ever-expanding. Media encompasses all information, art, and entertainment and includes Internet search engines, social media, news, gaming, television, music, film, streaming services, and advertising. Today, the top media companies are: Apple ($2.74 trillion), Disney ($238.21 billion), Comcast ($213.75 billion), Netflix ($152.77 billion), AT&T ($140.11 billion), and Sony ($114.10 billion).[14] To no surprise, each of the companies is WEF aligned.

If there is any industry that has dealt in misinformation, lies, propaganda, and suppression of the truth, it is the media! From creating our newsfeeds to affecting election outcomes, the media is the most powerful means of propaganda and social programming.

---

14 Shobhit Seth, "The World's Top Media Companies," https://investopedia.com, updated April 14, 2022.

The mainstream modern media, which exists through airwaves and frequencies, is certainly under the influence of Satan, who is aptly described as the "prince of the power of the air."

Internet and social media giants control information, news, and even what information pops up in searches. "Google has dominated the search engine market, maintaining a 92.47 percent market share as of June 2021."[15] This has allowed Google to literally control the flow of information and, thus, the narrative. Even when researching to write *Fight Like Heaven!*, information that was available one day had been taken down the next. There is no question that despite all of the information at our fingertips, the real facts and data are getting harder and harder to find.

If we recall the media coverage since the 2016 election, i.e., Donald Trump generally, the Russian Hoax particularly, the Durham Probe of the Clintons, Hunter Biden, and COVID-19, the anti-conservative narratives (or notable silence) were basically identical among all mainstream news platforms. And yet when the truth of these matters ultimately emerged, it was clear that the vast majority of the media was not objectively reporting the news but was actively involved in what can only be characterized as mind control and the deception of the American people. The fact that so many media conglomerates, organizations, and government agencies could so seamlessly conspire to create what is delivered as "the news" should send chills up the spine of every citizen.

We are in an information war, and the increase of technology has made this a techno-war. A war is underway, but many do not know that it is a war of propaganda to steal our freedoms and move us

---

15 Joseph Johnson, "Global Market Share of Search Engines 2010-2022," https://www.statista.com, March 1, 2022.

toward the New World Order. Our ideas, discussions, and even our faith have been censored and shadow banned by social media companies. Inherent in this power to silence is the power to utilize strong messaging to feed appetites, change values, and explore new ideas about sexuality, family, marriage, and especially to impact children. The media's goal is to get us all to think like they do and to embrace all of the values and causes that violate the Word of God.

With respect to children, the gaming industry is perhaps the most dangerous form of media because of the lifelike interations with sex and violence by the player. The newly launched Metaverse, Mark Zuckerberg's new empire, is taking role-play to a new level where its users create avatars with the ability to assault, rape, and do whatever they want in virtual spaces without consequences. What would have been considered in years past as hard-core pornography is now marketed to youth.

This strongly plays into the family failure in culture. Our children become the images they behold. There is a spirit/soul (mind, will, and emotions) connection to the body. Our minds can be tricked into believing propaganda, and it will have a brainwashing effect on our lives, health, and our children. Engaging in immoral behavior, whether with an avatar or in real life, creates brokenness and addictions.

Spiritual Warfare and Strategic Prayer:

➢ Take authority over and bind the prince of the air from operating in our media, and loose truth, wisdom, righteousness, and justice into our airwaves.

➢ Proclaim that Kingdom men and women will be raised up in all media outlets and have influence that will supersede that of the enemy.

➢ Declare that men and women of God would be free from censorship and exclusion from social media and that the Gospel would be shared boldly and unhindered.

➢ Pray that the media's fruitless deeds of darkness will be exposed.

➢ Pray that Christians will stand up against ungodly media with their voices and their dollars.

➢ Declare that social media outlets would be subject to legal standards in accordance with the First Amendment while protecting children from inappropriate and ungodly content.

Call to Arms:

➢ Lay down media and entertainment at the altar. Spend quality, uninterrupted, focused *time* with God, seeking His presence with your whole heart and meditating on His Word. This divine communion will bring you, among other things, joy, nourishment, protection, strength, wisdom, and discernment. The things of this world cannot compare.

➢ Get your news somewhere besides the mainstream media, which is now completely left stream. Consider the following resources, and be willing to pay for real news: *The Epoch Times* newspaper, The War Room with Steve Bannon, One America News (OAN), the Daily Wire, The Blaze, Newsmax, The Federalist, National Review, Breitbart, Zero Hedge, Townhall, the Washington Examiner, World Net Daily, Gab Trends, Washington Free Beacon, Life Site News, The Daily Signal, Drudge Report, Free Republic, American Thinker, Red State, The Gateway Pundit, FlashPoint, and Drenda on Guard.

➢ Boycott and redirect your consumption of ungodly media and organizations that support conservative censorship and globalist's ideologies, including: 1) Facebook, 2) Bank of America; use instead credit unions or state chartered banks in conservative states, 3) J.P. Morgan Chase (has stopped doing business with conservatives and de-platformed them), 4) Netflix (normalizes pedophilia); replace with Rumble, 5) Google (threatens and de-platforms conservatives); replace with Duck Duck Go, 6) Disney (voice of CCP); download Minno, a Christian app for children; watch old Disney CDs, 7) NBA (allowed Chinese instructors at their camps to abuse children); replace with playing ball with your son or daughter or friends, 8) Apple (pro-China, anti-American, and refused to release evidence of terrorists); replace with Samsung, Spotify, 9) The NFL (woke, anti-American); replace with college football or golf, 10) Levi Strauss (outspoken against the Second Amendment), 11) Nike (anti-American); and 12) Twitter.

➢ As King David, commit to "set no worthless thing before [your] eyes," including television, social media, and film. Ask yourself, "If I wouldn't allow my children to watch it, why am I watching it?"

➢ Be vigilant about the gaming and media to which your kids are exposed. There is no such thing as a 100% effective "parental control" other than your own eyes and ears. Most often, a technology parental control will alert you *after* the damage is already done. And a child can easily search for "ways to get around parental controls." While TikTok, Facebook, and Instagram are rated 12+, there is no limit to the vulgarity and ungodly content posted by users.

➢ Commit to getting off your phone, ipad, and tv screen and spending more time with your family outdoors, seeking adventure, and creating memories.

7

GOVERNMENT/POLITICS

It is for freedom that Christ has set us free. Stand firm, then, and do not let yourselves be burdened again by a yoke of slavery.
—Galatians 5:1 (NIV)

In the United States of America, the Constitution is the supreme law. In fact, it is the longest surviving government charter in the world. The Constitution has withstood the test of time because its authors had the wisdom and foresight to balance and separate federal and state governmental powers, to protect majority rule interests versus minority rights, and to ensure liberty and equality for all. This founding document sets forth the national framework of our government from the creation of the three branches of government to its 27 amendments. The fact that the Constitution itself created a government of the people, by the people, and for the people is demonstrated in its first three words: "We the People" (Constitution of the United States, Preamble).

Our original founding document, The Declaration of Independence, effectively broke America's bondage of slavery to the tyranny of

Great Britain. As our forefathers professed in this document, America was entitled to independence by "the Laws of Nature and Nature's God." It states:

> We hold these Truths to be self-evident, that all Men are created equal, that they are endowed by their Creator with certain unalienable Rights, that among these are Life, Liberty, and the Pursuit of Happiness—that to secure these Rights, Governments are instituted among Men, deriving their just Powers from the Consent of the Governed, that whenever any Form of Government becomes destructive of these Ends, it is the Right of the People to alter or to abolish it, and to institute new Government, laying its Foundation on such Principles, and organizing its Powers in such Form, as to them shall seem most likely to affect their Safety and Happiness.

According to this foundational document (The Declaration of Independence, July 4, 1776), truth is absolute; there is a Creator; we are all created equal; our rights are God-given; the right to life, liberty, and pursuit of happiness is immutable; government's function is to protect our rights; government exists by and for the people; destructive governments are subject to change or abolishment; God is intimately involved in the affairs of men; and America was founded on biblical principles.

Can you see how each of these precepts has been steadily eroding in our culture? From the notion that truth is relative to questioning the existence of a God to completely capsizing the role and power of government to control every facet of our daily lives, our modern-day political system would likely confound our Founding Fathers.

Most Americans have lived in freedom for so long, we take it for granted. While we are undeniably blessed to live in this country where we are still free to speak, worship, and prosper, the free America of yesterday and even today is not promised when we give our country over to those who do not honor God or His Word. Given our government's brazen infringement on our freedoms since the beginning of 2020, we can no longer afford to bury our heads in the sand to our own detriment and at the expense of future generations. Freedom of speech, personal expression, exercise of religion, bodily autonomy, education, and the ability to make a living all hang in the balance!

God, the Father gave Jesus Christ, the Son so that we could live in ultimate freedom! He paid the price with His precious blood. We cannot let ourselves be subject to the yoke of slavery, whether it be of man, sin, or Satan. We must stand on these biblical principles and enforce our "unalienable rights" which were "endowed by our Creator" to remain free and to raise our children to be free. It is the difference between sin or righteousness, sickness or health, death or life.

Spiritual Warfare and Strategic Prayer:

➢ Stand in the gap on behalf of the United State of America, and repent of all forms of wickedness, idolatry, and sin.

➢ God's Word says, "*Blessed is the nation whose God is the Lord, the people he chose for his inheritance*" (Psalm 33:12, NIV). As a nation, we exalt you, Jehovah, as our God and Lord.

➢ Acknowledge that, according to His Word, God makes nations great and destroys them. He enlarges nations and disperses them. Seek His blessing and ask that He restore, enlarge, and make great the United States of America.

➢ Cast down and drive out the principalities and strongholds of the Antichrist, Baal, Molech, and Ashtoreth, which have defiled our land, as well as the spirits of tyranny, totalitarianism, communism, genocide, infanticide, confusion, fear, poverty, slavery, and every other unclean thing from the United States of America.

➢ Declare Jesus Christ the King of the United States, and loose freedom, justice, godliness, righteousness, truth, and prosperity in our nation.

➢ Ask the Lord, who removes kings and sets up kings, to promote Kingdom men and women to attain positions of political authority in this country and replace those who would advance the enemy's agenda.

➢ Declare that the Constitution will be upheld and enforced in its entirety and that the rule of law, which provides that laws be consistently and equally applied, will be restored.

➤ Pray for righteous laws to be passed by our legislators and that our judges will administer justice in accordance with God's Word.

Call to Arms:

➤ Read and study the Constitution and The Declaration of Independence.

➤ Keep abreast of current events via reliable news sources as suggested in chapter six. Watch and subscribe to Drenda on Guard!

➤ Find out who your federal, state, and local representatives are, and actively advocate for godly laws and political action. Make calls, send emails, and share your views on their social media pages.

➤ Run for office or sign up to volunteer for another believer's political campaign.

➤ Get involved in your local city and neighborhood councils and school boards. What happens in the local community impacts the nation.

➤ Study candidates' platforms, and then vote for the men and women who represent the Kingdom of God.

8

EDUCATION

Then Jesus told His disciples... "For what will it profit a man if he gains the whole world and forfeits his soul? Or what shall a man give in return for his soul?"

—Matthew 16:24a-26 (ESV)

School is no longer about reading, writing, and arithmetic but social engineering and political agendas. Prayer and God were removed from schools in 1962. Since then, history has been rewritten, and God and the faith of our foundations have been removed from our American history. We knew that our government and schools had hit rock bottom when parents' involvement in their children's education was deemed by the Biden administration to be "terrorist behavior" and they summoned the FBI! While public schools have been teaching our children numerous ungodly doctrines for decades, e.g, that our ancestors crawled out of the swamp and we evolved from apes, they are now pushing the unimaginable on our children—gender identity and sexuality on five-year-olds.

For example, state boards of education provide kindergarten teachers with books advocating that sex is "assigned" at birth and introduce five-year-olds to terms like "trans, genderqueer, non-binary, gender fluid, transgender, gender neutral, agender, neutrois, bigender, third gender, two-spirit…."[16] Teachers unions have convened meetings advising teachers on effective methods for undermining parents, conservative communities, and school principals on issues of gender identity and sexual orientation, which involves surveilling students' conversations for the purpose of inviting them to LGBTQ clubs without their parents' knowledge or consent. "The Genderbread Person" is now a commonly used craft for teaching kids how to identify the various LGBTQ identities.[17] Similarly, "The Gender Unicorn," created by Trans Student Educational Resources, is being used to teach children about sex and gender identity.[18]

In Michigan, a school superintendent was petitioned by students to put litter boxes in school restrooms to accommodate kids identifying themselves as "furries." When the superintendent's potential plans were reported at a recorded school board meeting, the video went viral, sparking parental outrage and public disgust. Predictably, the superintendent denied the allegations as fake news, but the genie was already out of the bottle.

Many parents have been conditioned that it's normal to offer their children this ungodly educational brainwashing. Christian parents act shocked when their children reject God—but what do they expect when they've turned their children over to be raised by the world? Jesus said, "*The student is not above the teacher, but everyone*

16 Brook Pessin-Whedbee, *Who Are You? The Kid's Guide to Gender Identity*, Jessica Kingsley Publishers, Philadelphia, PA, 2017.
17 https://www.itspronouncedmetrosexual.com/2018/10/the-genderbread-person-v4
18 https://transstudent.org/gender

who is fully trained will be like their teacher" (Luke 6:40, NIV). Do you want your child to become like his or her teacher with values that are antagonistic to the Bible? Or do you want to be the primary teacher and influencer over your child's life? It's your decision alone.

Higher education is wrought with the same perils but with a much higher price tag. Universities and college campuses have been infiltrated with anti-God, anti-democracy, Marxist ideologies since the 1960s. The biggest cost for professing Christians is a study showing that roughly 70 percent of high school students entering college claiming to be born again abandon their faith after college.[19] This is a cost that is too high to pay!

According to the Education Data Initiative, a team of researchers whose mission is to collect data and statistics about the US education system, the ultimate price of the average bachelor's degree may be as high as $400,000![20] Despite the enormous expense, the old adage, "Go to college and get a good job" no longer applies today. Unless the skill a student wants to perform requires a degree, many degrees offer no advantage. We need to rethink education and invest in skills rather than ideologies taught in universities.

We should prepare youth by giving them a strong foundation in God's Word, developing their character—alongside the basics of reading, writing, and arithmetic—and exploring science from a biblical worldview. The final step is apprenticeship, vocational, or higher education as their God-given giftings become evident. When we seek a vocation for ourselves or our children based strictly on

19 Vaneetha Rendall Risner, "Will You Lose Your Faith in College?" https://www.desiringgod.org, August 23, 2018.

20 Melanie Hanson, "Average Cost of College and Tuition," https://www.educationdata.org, January 27, 2022.

money rather than on God's calling, we are not seeking first the Kingdom of God, and it misaligns priorities. Financial rewards follow seeking first the Kingdom of God. *"But seek first the kingdom of God and his righteousness, and all these things will be added to you"* (Matthew 6:33, ESV). Purpose is always more important than finances and will produce fulfillment, balanced living, *and* financial sufficiency.

Spiritual Warfare and Strategic Prayer:

➤ Break the strongholds of humanism, secularism, Marxism, homosexuality, gender confusion, pedophilia, mind control, and perversion permeating public schools and higher education.

➤ Demand that our government reestablish the free exercise of religion in our schools.

➤ Declare that our children will not be made to stumble or be hindered from knowing Jesus Christ by the indoctrination, instruction, groupthink, ungodly curricula, and agendas pushed by the public school system and colleges and universities.

➤ Pray that the fear of the Lord will be the basis of every action taken by public and Christian school teachers, administrations, coaches, and volunteers.

➤ Declare that Kingdom men and women will be raised up to be schoolteachers, administrators, school board members, and professors.

➢ Pray for increased faith, wisdom, and strength for parents to withdraw their children from the public school system and secular universities.

Call to Arms:

➢ Home education or Christian schools are no longer just optional; the risks are too high. Get before the Lord and ask Him how to train up your children in the way they should go in the area of their education.

➢ Know that if you disobey the call, there will be consequences that are greater than the price you would have paid to home educate or send your children to a Christian school.

➢ If you are a single parent or believe that your family requires a double income at this time, look into a career or job change that will allow you to work from home to facilitate homeschooling.

➢ If your children attend a Christian school, you must be vigilant about who is teaching your kids and what is being taught. You must be very engaged. Beware of wolves in sheep's clothing.

➢ Evaluate the culture's insistence that our children obtain a degree from a university in order to be successful. The Bible tells us to "count the costs," which include enormous debt, abandonment of faith, exposure to drugs and alcohol, and little to no increase in potential earnings.

➤ Consider college alternatives like apprenticeship, business ownership, Bible schools or Christian Universities, or online schools.

9

FAMILY

Your wife will be like a fruitful vine within your house; your children will be like olive shoots around your table.
—Psalm 128:3 (ESV)

Life began in a beautiful Garden, and the highest order of God's creation was humankind, male and female. God desired family so much that after He created Adam and Eve, *"then God blessed them, and God said to them, 'Be fruitful and multiply'"* (Genesis 1:28a, NKJV). In the Garden, God gave the first man and his companion and wife, Eve, everything they needed for life. God's plan was to enjoy close relationships with His family, His children, who would walk with Him for eternity.

But Satan conspired against God to get the allegiance of the first family. Man's decision to disobey God's Word brought the curse upon their lives. When confronted by God, Adam would blame his wife and God, "This woman You gave me told me to eat, so I did." Their son Cain would murder his brother Abel, consumed with jealousy and sibling rivalry. God's design of family quickly turned into brokenness and devastation.

Fast forward to the evolution of the American family. The destruction of the traditional family was the number one place of assault, removing the protecting force of parents guarding children in the home. The strong family values of the 40s and 50s gave way to the sexual rebellion and promiscuity of the 60s, developing a strong divorce culture. Today, the US has the world's highest rate of children living in single parent households. One-fourth of children live with a single parent due to a decline in marriage rates and a rise in births outside of marriage. And adult children, ages 18-34, living with their parents in the US is at a whopping 20 percent![21] Is it possible that these young adults are also modeling what they have been taught about marriage from their teachers, moms, and dads?

God began with a family, and His last order of business will begin with an awakening of family, starting with men. As Scripture says, God "*will turn the hearts of the parents to their children, and the hearts of the children to their parents*" (Malachi 4:6a, NIV). We need more good men. Men of God who are willing to love their wives and children are the greatest cure and, unfortunately, are in tremendous shortage. If men model what a loving husband and father looks like, good women will follow, and children will too. Men are the catalysts we need to right the wrongs, defend the homes, and drive out the darkness and clouds. When men rebel against God, so do women; and children rebel against parents. Our decisions always affect those under our leadership. We desperately need a revival of men to turn their hearts back to their wives, and especially to their children. There is no greater place to impact the culture than this mountain and no greater force than that of a father. Most of the brokenness in the culture could be healed by our Father, a good father. And men cannot be good without God.

---

21 Stephanie Kramer, "U.S. Has World's Highest Rate of Children Living in Single-parent Households," https://www.pewresearch.org, December 12, 2019.

God gave Adam and Eve another son after the loss of their son Abel to death. His name was Seth, and the lineage of Jesus Christ came through him. When it appeared all was lost, God sent His answer to cause the Son to shine and majesty to break forth in the world. A beautiful mountain appeared, the mountain of the Lord.

The nuclear family is the strength or downfall of any society and nation. As the family goes, so goes the nation. No mountain surpasses this one! Family has been wounded, but miraculous healing is possible. Women and children are yearning for godly men who represent our Father.

Spiritual Warfare and Strategic Prayer:

> ➤ Thank God that He restored the familial relationship between Him and His children whereby we can cry "Abba, Father!"

> ➤ Break strongholds of Ahab and Jezebel spirits and unclean spirits of division, strife, divorce, and fatherlessness within families.

> ➤ Pray for establishment of spiritual order in homes, where men are the heads, husbands love their wives just as Christ loved the church, wives respect their husbands, and children obey their parents in accordance with Ephesians 5:25-33 and 6:1.

> ➤ Pray that the winds of the Holy Spirit would sweep through the hearts of fathers, turning them back to their children.

➢ Call forth the prodigal sons and daughters to "come to [their] senses" and return to the Father (Luke 15:17, NIV)!

Call to Arms:

➢ *"Choose for yourselves this day whom you will serve"* (Joshua 24:15, NIV). Will you and your household serve the Lord?

➢ After your relationship with God, your relationship with your spouse has the highest priority. You must make time to grow and nurture it on a daily basis.

➢ Intercede for your spouse daily, and model what a godly man or woman looks like; do not try to assume the role of the Holy Spirit.

➢ Get your house in order. Do you follow the biblical order set forth in Ephesians 5:25-33 and 6:1? If not, ask the Holy Spirit to help you be the wife or husband He designed you to be.

➢ If your marriage is struggling, seek Christian counseling. The cost of divorce and a broken home far exceeds the price of a therapist.

➢ Take an inventory of your life, and ask the Lord to help you eliminate or replace those things that are interfering with your marriage or family. This includes your job, your kids' extracurricular activities, and even service. Consider working from home, limiting activities that demand your time away from your family, or choosing acts of service where your children can participate.

➤ Take a family vacation and fun trips outdoors. If cost is an issue, budget for it, which may include putting off expenditures like home improvements, new cars, or even small impulse purchases that quickly add up. Your children won't care about how nice your kitchen cabinets were, but they will care about the time you spent with them.

CONCLUSION

The mountains themselves are not evil, but because they are areas of influence corrupted by sin, they have been penetrated and honed to influence people, sadly, toward destruction. We have seen the collaboration of these areas of influence in alignment, where there is one agenda and all roads lead to the same destination. We are not to fear, but as 2 Corinthians 2:11a (NIV) says, be aware of the enemy's schemes *"…in order that Satan might not outwit us."*

It is no longer church as usual! God is calling us to be soldiers of the light, with love as our weapon and the Holy Spirit as our source of power and protection. If we will pray fervently over these areas, ask God for His strategies to have greater influence, and then add to our prayers commitment, action, and involvement, we can contend for the faith and reach into our personal spheres of influence to make a difference. Do not hesitate to share what you have learned in *Fight Like Heaven!*, this *A Call to Arms* guide, and Drenda on Guard with other believers and those who do not know Jesus. You have been called into the Kingdom of God for such a time as this. We can infiltrate the seven mountains again with the right mindset and reclaim lost or missed opportunities!

SALVATION

We are in a spiritual battle. You must be equipped. How? Well, the very first step to being properly equipped for the battle is to be saved.

What does it mean to be saved? It's simple.

God loves mankind so much that He sent His Son, Jesus to Earth to undo the work of the devil and to give His life to redeem and restore us back to God (1 John 3:8)—to save us and give us everlasting life with Him in heaven (John 3:16).

Salvation is about much more than just going to heaven when you die. It's about being translated out of the earth curse system of darkness that is ruled by Satan, who only wants to steal, kill, and destroy (John 10:10), and into the Kingdom of God, who gives life. It's having access to all of His great and precious promises while you still live on Earth.

You have a choice—stay in the kingdom of darkness, or be saved and live in the Kingdom of light.

And there is only one way to be saved.

> *Salvation is found in no one else, for there is no other name under heaven given to mankind by which we must be saved.*
> —Acts 4:12 (NIV)

> *Everyone who calls on the name of the Lord will be saved.*
> —Acts 2:21 (NIV)

Salvation is a free gift from God, and you can receive it just as you would receive a gift.

It's that easy. Just pray this simple prayer:

> *"Father, You said in the Bible that if I call on the name of Jesus, You will receive me, make me brand new on the inside, fill me with Your Holy Spirit, and teach me how to live life the Kingdom way. Today, let my name be recorded in heaven and that I called on the name of Jesus.*
>
> *Jesus, today, be my Lord and Savior. I receive Your goodness.*
>
> *Lord, based on your Word, I am now Your son/daughter and a citizen of Your Kingdom. I receive all of Your great and precious promises. I thank You for all of it, Lord. Amen."*

If you have prayed this prayer today, please reach out to us at info@faithlifenow.com so that we can celebrate with you.

There's no doubt warfare is happening in our culture.

How should you handle warfare?

How can you know the right decisions to make for your family, freedom, country, and faith?

What is your purpose for being here at this time, and what can you do?

Are we really living in the last days?

Get the answers to these urgent questions and much more in Drenda Keesee's powerful, best-selling book, *Fight Like Heaven! A Cultural Guide to Living on Guard.*

Join Drenda as she identifies the Seven Mountains of Influence the Antichrist spirit has invaded—religion, economy/business, health/medicine, media/entertainment, government/politics, education, and family. She leaves no stone unturned as she uncovers and exposes the enemy's shocking last days' agendas to deceive, enslave, impoverish, and kill God's most prized creation—people—while taking particular aim at destroying our children from the inside out.

Discover how you can stand up and fight the "war on God" as a believer and find peace and provision above this world's chaotic systems.

Get equipped to fight like heaven, kick hell out, and take back these mountains for the Kingdom of God!

Get your copy of *Fight Like Heaven! A Cultural Guide to Living on Guard* today by going to FightingLikeHeaven.com or Drenda.com.

ORDER YOUR COPY OF *FIGHT LIKE HEAVEN!* TODAY!

ABOUT DRENDA

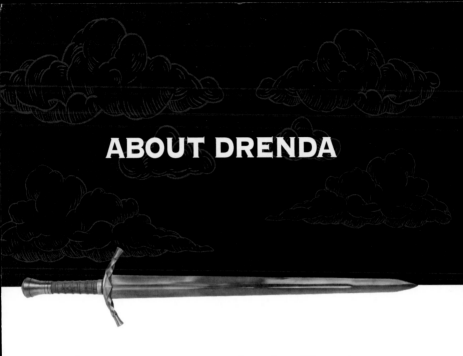

Drenda Keesee is an international speaker, life coach, pastor, businesswoman, best-selling author of several books, and television host of *Drenda* and the Drenda on Guard channel. Drenda is passionate about families, freedom, and finances and has made it her mission to expose the latest Antichrist agendas in order to equip believers to live in victory and without fear in these appointed times.

Drenda and her husband of 40 years, Gary Keesee, are the founders and senior pastors of Faith Life Church, which has campuses in New Albany and Powell, Ohio. They are also the founders of Faith Life Now, which reaches millions of people across the globe with the Good News of the Gospel through television shows, radio, worldwide conferences, online platforms, books, and teachings. Both ministries distribute Bibles, support churches and ministries in multiple nations, provide stable and nurturing environments for expectant mothers, victims of sex trafficking, and others in transition homes, facilitate the translation of Faith Life Now's books and teachings, and much more.

Drenda created The Happy Life, a mentorship program that includes video teachings, study materials, and The Happy Life Social app—a refreshing Kingdom alternative to other social media options—where women go for encouragement and build community.

In addition to her graduate studies at Oral Roberts University, Drenda received a Master's Degree in Christian Counseling from Logos University and an honorary Doctorate of Divinity from CICA International University and Seminary.

Drenda and Gary call Ohio home and enjoy spending as much time as possible with their five adult children and their spouses and their eleven grandchildren.